Date Due

AUG 3 0 '00			
MAR 0 3 00			
MAR 2 1 00			
APR 22 00			
FEB 2 8 00			
MAY 17 00			
JUN 19 0			
MAY 31 0			
MAY 28 05			

5/99

**Jackson
County
Library
Services**

**HEADQUARTERS
413 W.Main
Medford, Oregon 97501**

WIDE WORLD

PEOPLE *of the*
RAIN FORESTS

Anna Lewington and Edward Parker

RSVP
RAINTREE
STECK-VAUGHN
PUBLISHERS
The Steck-Vaughn Company
Austin, Texas

WIDE WORLD

PEOPLE *of the* **GRASSLANDS**
PEOPLE *of the* **DESERTS**
PEOPLE *of the* **ISLANDS**

PEOPLE *of the* **MOUNTAINS**
PEOPLE *of the* **POLAR REGIONS**
PEOPLE *of the* **RAIN FORESTS**

Cover: A Belaga-Kenyab woman from Sarawak, Malaysia, collecting medicinal rain forest plants

Title page: Children in the Philippines at the window of their reed hut, built with palms and other rainforest materials

This page and Contents page: An area of tropical rain forest in the Amazon region of South America

Published by Raintree Steck-Vaughn Publishers, an imprint of Steck-Vaughn Company

Library of Congress Cataloging-in-Publication Data
Lewington, Anna.
People of the rain forests / Anna Lewington.
    p.   cm.—(Wide world)
    Includes bibliographical references and index.
    Summary: Descibes the geography, plant and animal life, mineral resources, destruction, and environmental protection of the world's rain forests and how people live in this ecosystem.
    ISBN 0-8172-5061-1
    1. Rain forest people—Juvenile literature.
    2. Rain forests—Juvenile literature.
    3. Rain forest ecology—Juvenile literature.
    [1. Rain forests. 2. Rain forest ecology. 3. Ecology.]
    I. Parker, Edward, 1961–. II. Title. III. Series.
    GN394.L49 1998
    577.34—dc21   97-38626

Printed in Italy. Bound in the United States.
1 2 3 4 5 6 7 8 9 0 0 03 02 01 00 99

Contents

Introduction

The world's rain forests are often thought of as wild, mysterious places full of giant plants and dangerous animals. However, people have lived in rain forests for hundreds of thousands of years, and today they are home to a population of about 140 million. Rain forest people live in settlements ranging from traditional rain forest villages to huge cities.

Rain Forest Facts

Biggest rain forest: Amazon, South America
Wettest rain forests: Hawaii and Cameroon: over 200 in. (6 m) rain a year
Area covered by tropical rain forest: 3.2 million sq. mi. (8.5 million sq. km)
Area covered by temperate rain forest: 37–50 million acres (15–20 million hectares)

Rain forest people

Rain forest people come from a variety of racial backgrounds and have many different lifestyles. Some are called indigenous or tribal people. They are the descendants of the very first people who lived in rain forests thousands of years ago. Many indigenous people have very traditional lifestyles, hunting and growing the food that they need. Some rain forest dwellers are migrants, who have moved to the rain forest in search of land where they can grow enough food to feed their families. Others move to rain forests looking for jobs in industries like mining, logging, and cattle ranching.

A Kayapo Indian boy from ▶ the Amazon rain forest in Brazil

Rain forest destruction

Rain forest populations are increasing, but the rain forests themselves are being destroyed, as they are cut down for logging or to make room for crops, roads, settlements, and cattle ranches. Both indigenous and more recent rain forest peoples are living in a changing environment, and their future is uncertain.

A worker on an oil well in the forest of Gabon, ▶ West Africa. Oil is one of many resources in the rain forests that provide work for people.

▼ Caracas, the capital of Venezuela in South America, is a huge city surrounded by rain forest.

What Is a Rain Forest?

Rain forests are forests that grow in constantly wet conditions. Generally, forests that have more than 80 in. (2,000 mm) of rain (moisture) evenly spread throughout the year are considered to be rain forests.

Rain forests can be divided into two main types: tropical and temperate. Because there are so many different types of rain forests, even experts find it difficult to say where one kind of rain forest stops and another begins.

Tropical rain forests

Tropical rain forests are hot and wet. They can be found around the equator, between the Tropics of Cancer and Capricorn. About 90 percent of the world's tropical rain forests are found in the Amazon region of South America and in Central Africa and Southeast Asia.

▼ This map shows the main areas where the world's rain forests are located.

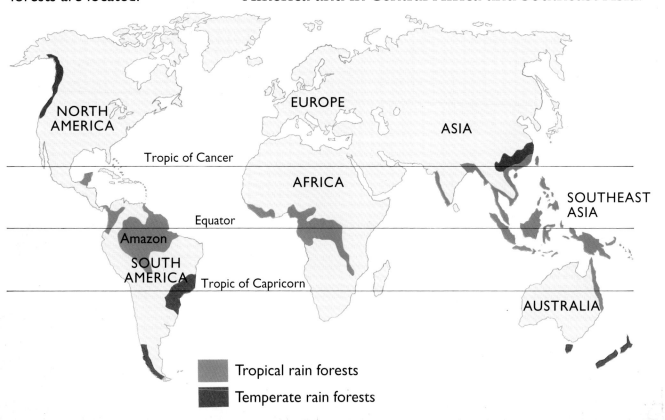

Tropical rain forests

Temperate rain forests

In the flooded forest of ▶ Brazil, in the upper Amazon, people organize their lives to fit the seasons.

Tropical rain forests are often divided into two main types: hot, humid lowland forests and cooler, damper montane forests, which are found above 3,000 ft. (900 m). Examples of lowland forest include flooded forest and mangrove forest.

Mangroves line one-fourth of the world's tropical coastlines. There are fifty-five different kinds of mangrove forests, covering an area of approximately 925 sq. mi. (2,400 sq. km). Mangrove forests give coastlines vital protection from waves, and they provide a sheltered environment where thousands of water creatures breed.

▼ The Amazon rain forest is the world's largest single area of rain forest, covering large expanses in countries like Venezuela.

Tropical Treasure Houses

Tropical rain forests are famous for their amazing variety of plant and animal life. Although they cover only six percent of the earth's surface, tropical rain forests are home to more than half of the world's animal and plant species. In a typical 4-sq.-mi. (10-sq.-km) patch of forest, scientists expect to find 1,500 species of flowering plants, 750 kinds of trees, 400 bird species, and more than 150 types of butterflies.

▼ Rain forest dwellers have used plants as medicines for centuries. This Belaga-Kenyab woman, in Sarawak, Borneo, is collecting a plant used to treat fevers.

Temperate rain forests

Temperate rain forests lie north and south of the tropics, where the rainfall is just as high but the temperature is cooler. Temperate rain forests can be found in southern Chile and along the northwest coast of North America, almost as far north as the Arctic Circle. Small but important areas of temperate rain forest can also be found in Tasmania, New Zealand, and even China.

Climate and lifestyle

Rain forests are very wet and some have heavy rain almost every day. Because of this heavy rainfall, rain forest people often build their houses on stilts to keep them above the wet ground. In one part of the Amazon rain forest, the water level of the rivers and lakes can rise by 43 ft. (13 m) in the wet season. The heavy rain can even wash away roads.

Cities in tropical rain forest regions have fewer trees to provide shade and absorb heat. Many offices and homes there have air-conditioning systems to keep the buildings cool in the fierce heat of the sun.

The importance of rain forests

Rain forests are vitally important to every human being on earth. They provide timber, food, medicine, and many raw materials that are vital to industries around the world. Rain forests also allow all life on earth to thrive by helping to maintain the balance of the gases in the atmosphere, which helps control the climate.

Disappearing Forests

More than half of the world's rain forest has disappeared in the last fifty years. Tropical rain forests are being destroyed at a rate of about 55,000 sq. mi. (142,000 sq. km) per year. Temperate rain forests now cover less than half of their original area. It is estimated that, in about twenty years' time, the only large expanses of rain forest left will be found in the Congo and Amazon river basins.

▲ Typical tropical rain forest vegetation in Costa Rica

The red-eyed tree frog is one ▶ of thousands of animal species found in the world's rain forests.

▲ An Asmat man in Irian Jaya, Indonesia, fishing in a mangrove forest. Mangrove forests are rich in fish, which provide food for forest dwellers.

The 140 million people who live in, or close to, the world's rain forests benefit directly from their environment. The plants provide shade and absorb the heat of the sun, making tropical climates cooler. The roots of plants hold the soil together and absorb water, which helps prevent flooding during heavy rainstorms.

Rain forest resources

One of the most valuable features of the rain forests is their huge selection of plant life, which provide useful products such as food, timber, and rubber. Many of the plants are also valuable for their medicinal properties, and indigenous rain forest peoples have been using plants as cures for hundreds of years. Recently, scientists have begun exploring rain forests in search of new plants containing chemicals that might help solve medical problems such as AIDS or cancer. Drugs derived from rain forest plants are already in use. For example, the bark of one type of tree in Cameroon is collected in large quantities to produce an anticancer drug.

Besides plants and animal life, rain forests provide many natural mineral resources. Some of the world's largest sources of iron, gold, aluminum, copper, and oil are found under areas of rain forest. The economy of Nigeria has been helped enormously by the discovery of huge stores of oil under its rain forest, and in the Camisea region of the Peruvian Amazon, a new gas field has recently been discovered that holds an estimated 9.9 trillion cu. ft. (280 billion cu. m) of gas. Mining is big business and provides thousands of jobs, but it can also cause terrible damage and pollution in the rain forests.

▼ An iron-ore furnace in the Grande Carajas area of the Amazon rain forest, in Brazil

Crash Landing
In 1967, a helicopter flying over the Amazon rain forest in Brazil was forced to crash land on a hill. On board was a geologist. While he waited to be rescued, he investigated the rocks on the hill. He found that they were made of high-grade iron ore. This area, called the Grande Carajas, is the world's largest deposit of iron ore and is now a large mining area. It is estimated that 20 billion tons of iron ore exist there.

History of Rain Forest People

First people

It is thought that people first moved into rain forests about one million years ago. Some scientists think that these people came from savannah (grassland) areas surrounding the forests. Over tens of thousands of years, rain forest people became smaller in size as they adapted to their environment. Races of people who are small in stature are thought to be among the most ancient rain forest peoples and include the Pygmies of Africa, the so-called negritos of Asia, the Onge people of the Andaman Islands, and the Aeta of the northern Philippines.

Indigenous Peoples

There are hundreds of indigenous groups living in rain forests. In Brazil alone there are thought to be 140 groups, each with a different language and culture. Changes in the rain forests have led to the disappearance of many groups. It is thought that about 1,000 South American Indian groups have disappeared during the twentieth century alone.

There is evidence that people have lived in Amazonia for the last 15,000–20,000 years, but these forests have probably been inhabited for jmuch longer.

▼ This pyramid was built by the Mayan culture, which flourished in the rain forests of southern Mexico and Central America between A.D. 300 and A.D. 800.

A Tuli landowner in Papua ▶
New Guinea, in his garden of
medicinal plants. Rain forest
people have known about
medicinal plants for
thousands of years.

Colonists

At the end of the fifteenth century, Europeans began to explore the world, searching for "new lands" and for goods and resources to trade. By this time, the people of many different nations had already been traveling and trading with rain forest peoples for a very long time. For example, Indian and Chinese traders had been sailing between the rain forest islands of Southeast Asia for over a thousand years. Rain forest people themselves were also on the move. In Amazonia and Africa, rain forest communities traded with people from other areas.

Rain Forest City

The city of Belem in Brazil is on the Amazon River. In the eighteenth century, Belem was a small fishing settlement. Today, it is a huge city with a population of over one million. Belem's dramatic development began with the "rubber boom," which occurred between about 1890 and 1910. During these years, rubber from wild Amazonian trees was in great demand for the manufacture of tires for motor vehicles.

▼ The city of Belem is a wealthy port on the Amazon River. Goods such as lumber and Brazil nuts are exported from there.

14

The arrival of Europeans had a dramatic effect. In just a few decades, the populations of indigenous peoples were reduced sharply by new diseases brought from Europe and by slave labor and cruel treatment.
This happened in the Moluccas, or "Spice Islands," of Indonesia. The Moluccas were the source of spices such as cloves and nutmeg, which were highly profitable to the spice trade. The islands were colonized by the Portuguese at the end of the fifteenth century, and the colonists treated the indigenous people appallingly. The Banda Islands had a population of around 15,000 when the Portuguese arrived. Within a few years, this had fallen to just 1,000 because many islanders had been executed, sold as slaves, or had committed suicide.

Over the last 500 years, people from Europe and elsewhere have colonized many countries that contain rain forests and have brought different lifestyles to the forests. They have exploited resources such as lumber, rubber, minerals, spices, and oil, set up plantations and mines, built settlements, roads, and railroads, and introduced Christianity. More recently, migrants from within rain forest countries, as well as from abroad, have moved to rain forest areas.

▲ Gold mining in Brazil. The valuable mineral resources that first attracted European settlers to rain forest areas are still important to rain forest economies today.

The twentieth century

It has been during the twentieth century that the greatest changes to rain forests have taken place. Many new towns and cities have been built, providing modern facilities from shopping malls to hospitals and recreation complexes. Millions of people are still trying to escape poverty and overcrowding by migrating to rain forest areas in search of land on which to grow food. In some countries, like Brazil, government programs encourage people to move to the rain forests. Jobs in ranching, agriculture, mining, and logging attract workers from other areas to live in the rain forest.

▼ This family has recently arrived on the rain forest island of Kalimantan, Indonesia. They were moved from their home on the crowded island of Java, as part of the Indonesian government's Transmigration Program.

Transmigration

Since the 1950s, the Indonesian government has been carrying out an enormous project, moving millions of people from the overpopulated islands of Java and Bali to the Outer Islands. So far, nearly 7 million people, known as transmigrants, have been settled in Sumatra, Kalimantan, Sulawesi, Nusa Tenggara, and Irian Jaya.

This transmigration project is intended to ease the population pressure on Java and Bali and to encourage development in rain forest areas. But there have been many problems. The transmigrants burn huge areas of forest for farming, and many indigenous people have been forced off their land. In 1997, a massive disaster occurred on Kalimantan, when huge forest fires burned for several months, blocking out the sun and filling the air with smoke. The rains failed to arrive, and vast areas of rain forest were destroyed.

Snakes in the Night

A rubber tapper working in the Brazilian rain forest in 1908, wrote in his diary: "My main trouble now was boa constrictors [snakes]... visiting me pretty near every night.... They come crawling along noiselessly and roll their body up alongside the hammock laying their heads on one's chest, from time to time sticking their tongue in the corner of one's eye or mouth, then sticking their head, which is ice-cold, under one's armpit."

▼ Pictured in the 1890s, this group of Amazon rain forest Indians is typical of many who were captured by European colonists during the rubber boom and forced to work as slaves.

Work in Rain Forests

For most traditional rain forest peoples, work is not just one activity, but a number of activities related to getting food, raising their families, and looking after their homes.

Hunting and fishing

For many rain forest dwellers, hunting and fishing are the main ways of obtaining their own food—and perhaps some extra to sell. For example, in the markets of Lagos, the capital of Nigeria, "bush meat" from the rain forest is for sale every day.

▼ Two boys fishing in Indonesia, using scoop nets and a traditional trap made of rattan and bamboo fibers

Rain forest animals, such as the jaguar in Colombia and the crocodile in Africa, are also hunted for their skins. In parts of India, endangered sloth bears are hunted illegally so that parts of their bodies can be used for Chinese medicine.

In mangrove areas, such as the mouth of the Ganges River in Bangladesh and in coastal Ecuador, many people make their livings from catching fish and shellfish and farming shrimp. Fishing for salmon is traditional and is still important for peoples such as the Tlingit and the Haisla, of the northwest coast of North America.

▲ Children harvesting chili peppers in a typical rain forest garden in Nigeria

Rain forest gardens

Millions of rain forest people—whether indigenous or not—spend much of their time collecting wild foods and firewood and tending small gardens cut out of the forest. These rain forest gardens occur throughout the world. Usually, a small area of forest is cut down, and the branches and wood are burned. The wood ash that is left helps the crops grow. The area is then planted with many different crops, such as cassava (a root vegetable) in South America, yams (a vegetable similar to the potato) in tropical Africa, and corn in Central America. Bananas and other fruit trees such as mangoes are also planted.

Collecting rain forest products

Millions of people are employed in collecting, transporting, and processing products from rain forests. These products include raffia in Madagascar, jalapeño chili peppers in Central America, and swallowtail butterflies from Indonesia, which are sold to tourists. In Southeast Asia, the ropelike stems of rattan palms are collected all year round by local people. About half a million people make their living by harvesting and processing the rattan stems, which are used mostly to make furniture.

Longest Rattan Stem
The longest rattan stem found so far measured 800 ft. (244 m).

◀ This man has been gathering rattan cane from the rain forests of Kalimantan, in Indonesia.

Scientists

Scientists from many countries are at work in the rain forests of the world. Some are researching the indigenous peoples; others are studying the rain forest plants, animals, or minerals. Many are at work identifying plants, some of which may be used in medical research.

Scientists collecting and ▶ studying seeds and leaves for medical research in the rain forest of Papua New Guinea.

Collecting rain forest products to sell is now an essential way for many people to earn a small amount of money to help them survive. The working conditions are often bad and wages are very low. Much of the work is seasonal, and millions of people do this work for part of the year, before returning to their small farms and gardens. Seasonal products include Brazil nuts from Peru, Bolivia, and Brazil and edible caterpillars from West Africa. In Mexico, thousands of people leave their towns and villages in or near the rain forest in October, to spend three months collecting the sticky sap of the chicle tree, which is used to make chewing gum.

This man is making a sleeping mat ▶ out of raffia leaves in a rain forest village in Cameroon. Traditional crafts like this provide many rain forest people with money to live on.

▲ A worker at an oil palm plantation in Malaysia, loading palm fruit into containers, ready to be taken to the factory.

Working on plantations

In tropical rain forests, big businesses and landowners have set up large plantations, producing products such as African oil palm, rubber, coffee, pineapples, nutmegs, and cloves. Although plantations provide employment for both local people and migrants, the conditions and pay are usually very poor. For example, on rain forest tea plantations in China, rubber plantations in Malaysia, and oil palm plantations in West Africa, people must work long hours with just a few days off each year. Processing factories set up near plantations also provide employment, but working conditions inside are often hot and very uncomfortable.

A good example of a profitable plantation crop is African palm oil. Throughout West Africa, Southeast Asia, and South America, large plantations of African oil palm have been established in rain forest areas. The fruits and their seeds produce two kinds of oil, which are used in large quantities for a variety of products from crackers to perfume and soap. African oil palms are now the world's most important source of oils.

◀ A worker on a pineapple plantation on the Ivory Coast

▲ A cowboy in Brazil tending a herd of cattle on land that was once rain forest

Ranching and logging

Two industries that have had a big effect on rain forest areas are ranching and logging. Since the 1970s, large areas of rain forest in South and Central America have been cut down and burned to make way for cattle ranches. Most of these produce beef to supply wealthy countries such as the United States. Ranching earns a lot of money in rain forest areas, but it provides jobs for very few people, since most cattle herds can be tended by a small number of herders on horseback.

The activity of logging companies is having the greatest single effect on forests worldwide. Heavy machines do much of the felling and processing, but large numbers of people are employed. In Canada and Australia, foresters generally operate heavy machinery such as harvesters, cranes, and giant saws, but in places like Gabon and the Solomon Islands, people do many of the jobs by hand.

▼ Alaskan timber is floated down the river to this mill, where it is cut into planks or pulped to make paper.

Alaska
More than one-third of Alaska is forested, and running along the coast is an area of temperate rain forest containing some of the largest trees on earth. These forests are currently being cut down so that the logs can be sold to Asian countries, mainly Japan, to be used to make paper and plastics. Thousands of people work in the lumber industry, and Alaska exports around 16,000 cu. ft. (450,000 cu. m) of wood a year.

Transportation and Communications

Rain forests today still include some of the last truly wild places on earth. They have remained wild largely because they are difficult to travel in. The combination of dense vegetation, heavy rains, steep slopes, and swampy soils continues to create a barrier to rapid travel. In many rain forest areas of the world, traveling on foot is often the only way to get around.

Rivers as roads

Rivers have been, and still are, the most important highways in rain forests. For millions of rain forest people, canoes with motors or oars are an extremely important means of travel. Logging and mining companies, among others, often use huge boats to transport products out of the rain forest to ports and to factories.

▼ These Wayana Indian children from French Guiana travel to school by motorized canoe every day.

A boat arriving in Belem, Brazil, with a cargo of Brazil nuts for processing may have traveled 3,000 mi. (5,000 km) upstream by the time it arrives.

On large rivers, and for trips between rain forest islands, passenger ferries are widely used. A huge variety of other water craft are also used in rain forest areas, including hovercraft, motorboats, and even jet skis. There are a growing number of tourist boats on rain forest rivers, especially in tourist areas like parts of Thailand.

Traditional Boats

Many indigenous rain forest people still use hollowed-out tree trunks to make boats. The Maori of New Zealand and the Tlingit of Alaska make wooden boats that can be used on the ocean. In the Amazon and African rain forests, canoes are still made from tree trunks.

▲ Drying out a freshly carved canoe, made from the trunk of a rain forest tree

▼ A passenger ferry on the Amazon River in Brazil

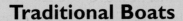

▲ Constructing a road through the Brazilian Amazon. The road will link the Brazilian cities of Manaus and Boa Vista with Venezuela.

Roads through the rain forest

Road travel is relatively new to rain forests. It is not easy to build and maintain roads in such hot, wet conditions. Heavy rains often wash away roads, and some are passable for only a few months of the year. In some rain forest areas, the roads have to be laid again after each rainy season. Most rain forest roads are still not paved.

Most people generally travel along roads on overcrowded buses or trucks. The operators of industries such as logging and mining often have to build their own roads to transport raw materials. It is usually only very wealthy people who travel by private car. A cheaper means of transportation is the bicycle.

Walkways in the Trees

Some scientists working in rain forests use an ingenious way to travel among the treetops. Cables suspended between the larger trees support walkways in the air. This enables scientists to walk between the tops of the large trees, sometimes higher than 250 ft. (75 m) above the ground.

A walkway in the treetops of the rain ▶ forest in Borneo, Malaysia

Maintaining roads in rain forest areas is very difficult because the forest vegetation grows so quickly. Roads can become overgrown in only a few months if not looked after. Even insects like ants can make roads impassable. Some kinds of ants look for flat areas of soft earth in which to make their underground nests, which can be 300 ft. (100 m) across. They often choose rain forest roads, which sometimes cave in because of the enormous network of chambers and tunnels under the road. This has even happened to the huge Trans-Amazonian Highway in Brazil.

The children of workers on an oil palm ▶ plantation in Cameroon, walking to school. Roads are often built by large companies, to provide transportation for crops, logging, and industrial products.

Railroads

There are railroads in various rain forest areas of the world, but they are much less common than roads and generally much less important than rivers for transporting passengers. Many railroads were built to transport raw materials. One of the newest and most ambitious railroads cuts through the rain forest of Gabon in Africa, linking the capital city of Libreville with the important mining town of Franceville.

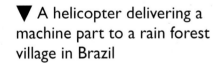

▲ Local people and tourists waiting for a train that runs from San Antonio to Porto Velho in the Amazon

▼ A helicopter delivering a machine part to a rain forest village in Brazil

Air travel

Travel by plane and helicopter has opened up areas of rain forest that could once be reached only by weeks of walking or boat travel. For example, travel between the rain forest islands of the Solomons is only possible by plane or boat. Dotted across the world's rain forests there are now thousands of small, unpaved runways where light aircraft can land. Geologists from oil and mining companies often travel to remote areas by helicopter or small aircraft to carry out surveys. Tourists, missionaries, and government officials all make use of this form of travel. For most rain forest people, however, air travel is too expensive.

In the coastal rain forest areas of New Zealand and Tasmania, the only quick way to travel is by helicopter. In the forests of New Zealand, some large trees that have been cut for their lumber are airlifted out because there are no logging roads.

▼ Asian elephants at work in the logging industry of Lampang Province, Thailand. The Asian elephant is an endangered species.

Homes and Settlements

▲ The roof of this house is thatched with palm leaves.

▼ A woman preparing bush meat outside her mud house in a rain forest village in Cameroon.

Traditional homes

Indigenous rain forest people live in many different sorts of traditional buildings. The number of people who live in each house and the kinds of settlements they make up also vary.

Some of the smallest and simplest dwellings are the huts used for part of the year by the Baka Pygmies of Cameroon. These individual family huts are made by using a framework of small branches, covered with overlapping leaves. The Penan of Sarawak are another nomadic people who use simple shelters that can be abandoned and rebuilt as required. The Mehinaku Indians of Brazil, on the other hand, build huge, dome-shaped houses up to 130 ft. (40 m) long, with grass roofs. The men of many different families work together to build each house, which will have room for about 30 people to live comfortably inside.

The materials used to build traditional shelters vary from forest to forest, depending on what is locally available. For example, in the Nigerian rain forest some people live in houses with clay walls, whereas in the cool rain forests on the Pacific coast of North America, planks cut from giant trees such as cedars are used to make some traditional houses.

Longhouses

Longhouses are the traditional homes of the Dyak peoples of Borneo and can house up to 100 families. Each family has its own door and a private area inside with storerooms, a sleeping area, and a kitchen at the back. The front of the longhouse has a wide, open, porchlike area running its length where social activities take place. Longhouses are often built almost entirely of plentiful local bamboo.

▼ A Dyak longhouse in Borneo

▲ Village children playing in front of their stilt huts in a village in the Philippines

Making a Mbuti Hut

The Mbuti Pygmies live in the rain forest of Central Africa. The women make their huts by fixing a ring of young trees in the ground and twining the tops together. Branches are then woven into the framework, and layers of leaves are attached to make the hut waterproof. Finally, the huts are secured with larger branches so they will not blow away in strong winds.

Many rain forest houses are built on stilts. Wooden stilt houses are often found in coastal areas, or where there is likely to be flooding. In the Philippines, the stilt houses of the Badajao people stand in sheltered coastal waters and are connected by slender poles. On dry land, raising a house above the ground provides rain forest dwellers with protection against wild creatures and separates them from domestic animals such as pigs and chickens.

New houses

Today, people who are not traditional rain forest dwellers frequently build houses that are unsuitable for the local conditions. These often have cement walls and corrugated iron roofs, which heat the inside of the house during the day. When heavy rain falls on the metal roof, the sound inside the house is deafening. Many indigenous forest people are now living in these houses, too, because they have been forced to change their way of life. This kind of house is the most common for people in towns and cities in rain forest areas. In places like Manila in the Philippines, or Cairns in Australia, wealthy people live in houses or apartment buildings that are well built, with air-conditioning to keep them cool.

A few buildings, such as those built specially for eco-tourists, use the latest technology to provide comfortable living quarters without damaging the environment. This involves using solar power, collecting rainwater for drinking, and using special toilets to protect the environment.

▼ Modern apartment buildings in a clearing in the Amazon rain forest, near the city of Belem

Inside rain forest houses

Indigenous rain forest people generally use materials that they gather themselves to build and furnish their homes. These may include strong, rot-resistant timbers, strips of bark and thatch made from palm leaves. Fibers stripped from palm and other leaves, as well as vines and canes are used to make things like mats, baskets, and sieves. Hammocks made of cotton or other plant fibers are popular throughout Central and South America. They are much cooler than beds and are just as popular in towns and cities as they are in remote forest areas.

▼ A young girl swings in a hammock in a mangrove village in southern Mexico.

Leisure and Tourism

Many rain forest people have to work very hard most of the time, but when they have some free time they may spend it in a variety of ways. For the wealthy, the number of recreational activities is endless: water skiing, the movies, yachting, concerts, shopping, and restaurants. Poorer people do not usually have much free time. A day off is likely to be spent sleeping or just being with the family. Most people working in the rain forest enjoy celebrating religious holidays, watching television, and playing soccer.

Mayan Basketball

Over 1,000 years ago, the Mayas in Mexico played a game called ollamaltitzli, *which was similar to the modern game of basketball. The players kept the ball off the ground, using their feet and elbows. The idea of the game was to get the ball through a stone hoop set high on a wall.*

▼ A group of men playing a game of checkers in the rain forest city of Belem, Brazil

Traditional pastimes

Leisure time, as we know it, would be a puzzle to many traditional rain forest people. Time not spent gardening or preparing food, for example, is often used for making useful tools, playing with the children, or telling stories. Traditional activities include swimming, making pots, and wrestling. Soccer is also becoming very popular.

▼ For many rain forest children, there are few toys. These boys in the Philippines have a homemade bicycle.

▲ A game of soccer on the Cook Islands of Polynesia.

Television and radio

In all but the remotest parts of rain forests, it is possible to watch television and listen to the radio. Some rain forest towns in Alaska, Mexico, and Australia have their own local television and radio stations, but most now have either cable or satellite television. In wealthy villages, every house may have a television set. In the poorest parts of many rain forests, a town's restaurants are often the only places where people can watch television.

Sports

Traveling through a rain forest in Central America or West Africa, one may see soccer fields close to many villages. Soccer is very popular and is often included in school activities. Many other sports are also popular. For example, villages in the mangrove forests of Mexico usually have soccer fields and volleyball courts; in Bangladesh the most common women's sport is badminton. Because of the climate and landscape, swimming is popular throughout the world's rain forests. It is a practical skill as well as a pastime, and rain forest children usually learn to swim at an early age.

Festivals and music

Many religious festivals are celebrated in rain forest villages and towns, and celebrations and festivals are held to mark important events. On particular days, the whole community joins together to mark an important event or to give thanks for a good harvest. These celebrations are very happy occasions, with music and dancing, and can last for many days. Women often work together to supply food and drink for a whole village, as well as for visiting guests.

Ju Ju Men
The Ju Ju man can be seen at many traditional West African ceremonies. He is usually dressed in a one-piece body suit so that the other villagers do not know who he is. In Cameroon and Nigerian rain forest communities, the Ju Ju man of the Ekpe religion performs dances as the leopard spirit.

▼ Four men of the Yagua people of Colombia playing traditional drums

A Ju Ju man dressed as a leopard spirit in a remote ▶ rain forest village in Cameroon

▲ For those who can afford them, there are now modern recreational activities, such as jet skiing, in rain forests.

Recreation for workers

Some of the best sports facilities in rain forests are those found at remote oil wells, power plants, and mines. In the Brazilian rain forest, at the massive Tucurui Dam project, an entire town was built specially for the workers. It is fenced with barbed wire to keep local people out, but inside there are bars, movies, swimming pools, and tennis courts.

At remote oil drilling platforms in places like Sarawak, in Malaysia, recreation facilities such as tennis and squash courts and a social club have to be built before engineers will agree to work on a new drilling platform.

Tourism

Over the last twenty years, the number of tourists visiting rain forest areas has been growing. It is now popular to visit rain forests on vacation or as part of a luxury cruise. Hotels in rain forests even organize treks to see wildlife and traditional ways of life.

Tourism provides employment in rain forest regions, and in some areas it has become the main form of employment. However, it has led to a change in lifestyle for many rain forest people. Among the advantages of tourism are that it increases people's awareness of the lifestyle of indigenous rain forest people and of the fragile environment. However, some indigenous peoples resent that some traditional villages now exist only as places for tourists to visit.

▼ Tourists on a guided trek in the rain forest of Ecuador. Eco-tourism brings visitors to rain forest areas to learn about the forest and its plants, animals, and indigenous peoples.

Work in Tourism

Millions of people are already employed in tourism in rain forest areas, and it is predicted that the number of jobs will continue to increase. Jobs range from work in hotels and restaurants, to acting as guides, showing visitors rare rain forest animals and plants.

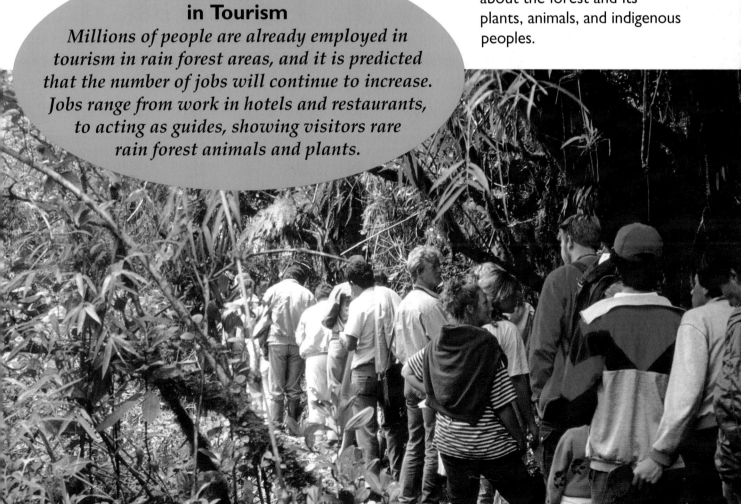

The Future

Rain forests are important to everyone in the world, whether they live in the rain forests or not. But they are disappearing at an alarming pace. The world's population is increasing at a rate of one million people every four days. This has two effects on rain forests: more rain forest products are needed to support the population, and increasing numbers of people are moving to rain forest areas. All this has increased the destruction of the forests. Urgent action is required to slow the loss of rain forests if they are to survive for long into the twenty-first century.

Protecting the forests

There are many ways of protecting the rain forests. National parks have been set up in countries like Australia, Cameroon, and Thailand, to control the use of the forests and to protect the plants and animals. There is also growing pressure for the proper management of rain forests. This means taking products such as lumber, spices, and nuts without seriously damaging the forest.

▼ Penan people in Malaysia blocking a road used by a logging company. Many Penan people have been arrested and put in prison for trying to stop loggers from destroying their homes.

These children in Cameroon ▶
are learning about the forest where
they live so that they can protect it
for the future.

International interest

People all around the world are
becoming more aware of the
need to preserve the rain forests.
Campaigns have been organized
to stop deforestation and to get
large companies and
governments to recognize the
rights of rain forest people.

Fighting for the forests

Many rain forest people are
trying desperately to save their
homes and their livelihoods. The
struggle has sometimes ended in
violence. In 1989, Chico Mendes
was killed because he organized
protests against the destruction
of the rain forest of the
Brazilian Amazon.

The way forward

Environmental groups are
campaigning to make sure that
rain forests are protected. They
also want the remaining forests
to be managed so that they are
not destroyed. Then the rain
forests can go on to provide raw materials for future
generations. Many of the groups help schoolchildren
learn more about the rain forests by printing leaflets and
booklets for schools.

Glossary

Atmosphere The gases that surround the earth (or other planets).

Bush meat A term widely used in Africa referring to meat from wild animals.

Colonized Occupied by people who have moved from somewhere else.

Deforestation The clearing of trees from a forest area.

Descendants People who are descended from previous generations.

Economy The financial system of a country.

Eco-tourism Ecologically responsible tourism that tries to bring tourists and nature together without harming or disturbing the environment.

Endangered At risk of dying out.

Environment Our surroundings, including the landscape, animals, and plants.

Equator An imaginary line around the earth, midway between the North and South poles.

Flooded forest A forest that is flooded permanently or at certain times of the year.

Geologist A person who studies rocks and the landscape.

Hammock A canvas or rope bed that hangs from cords at each end.

Indigenous Belonging originally or naturally to a particular place.

Mangrove forest Evergreen forest found along some tropical coastlines and in swamps.

Migrants People who move from their homes to another area or country.

Mineral A substance such as oil, coal, or metal that is obtained by mining.

Missionaries People who travel to places in order to spread a religious message.

Nomadic Constantly on the move, having no fixed home.

Ore A rock from which useful metal [iron ore] can be obtained.

Plantations Areas in which single crops are planted, often in rows.

Pollution Damage to the environment.

Raw materials The materials from which manufactured goods are made.

Solar power Power generated from the heat of the sun.

Species A group of plants or animals of the same type that share similar characteristics.

Temperate A mild or moderate climate.

Tropics The area, between the Tropics of Cancer and Capricorn, which has high temperatures and rainfall.

Further Information

Books to read

Gallant, Roy A. *Earth's Vanishing Forests*. New York: Simon and Schuster Children's Group, 1992.

Ganeri, Anita. *Forests* (Habitats). Austin, TX: Raintree Steck-Vaughn, 1996.

Goodman, Billy. The Rain Forest. Boston: Little Brown & Co., 1992.

Landau, Elaine. *Tropical Rain Forests Around the World* (First Books). Danbury, CT: Franklin Watts, 1991.

Lewington, Anna. *Atlas of Rain Forests*. Austin, TX: Raintree Steck-Vaughn, 1997.

Mason, Paul, ed. *Atlas of Threatened Cultures*. Austin, TX: Raintree Steck-Vaughn, 1997.

Miller, Christina and Louise A. Berry. *Jungle Rescue: Saving the New World Tropical Rain Forests*. New York: Simon and Schuster Children's Group, 1991.

Morrison, Marion. *The Amazon Rain Forest and its People*. Austin, TX: Raintree Steck-Vaughn, 1993.

Sayre, April P. *Tropical Rainforest* (Exploring Earth's Biomes). New York: 21st Century Books, 1994.

Siy, Alexandra. *The Amazon Rainforest* (Circle of Life). Parsippany, NJ: Silver Burdett Press, 1992.

Useful addresses

Friends of the Earth
1025 Vermont Avenue NW
Suite 300
Washington, D.C. 20005-6303
(202) 783-7400

Reforest the Earth
2218 Blossomwood Court NW
Olympia, WA 98502

Earth Living Foundation
P.O. Box 188
Hesperus, CO 81326
(970) 385-5500

The World Rainforest Movement
Chapel Row
Chadlington
Oxfordshire OX7 3NA
Tel: 01608 676691

World Wildlife Fund
1250 24th Street NW
P.O. Box 96555
Washington, D.C. 20077-7795

Forest Stewardship Council
RD 1 Box 182
Waterbury, VT 05676
(800) 244-6257

Picture acknowledgments
The publisher would like to thank the following for allowing their pictures to be used in this book: Bruce Coleman 20; Environmental Images 44; Getty Images *Title page*, 5, 7, 9 (both), 21 (top), 25, 37; Impact 30 (bottom), 40; Panos 16, 23, 32 (top), 33, 34, 38, 41 (left), 42; Edward Parker 7 (top), 21 (bottom), 24, 29 (bottom), 32 (bottom), 36, 41 (right); Planet Earth 13; South American Pictures 14, 17, 26, 27 (top), 30 (top); Still Pictures *Cover*, Chapter openers, 4, 5 (top), 8, 10, 11, 15, 18, 19, 22, 28, 29 (top), 31, 39, 43, 45; Wayland Picture Library 12.

Index

Numbers in **bold** refer to photographs.